BEFORE YOU START

This book contains instructions to make your own rocket. Before you start, check out the warnings below and follow the advice to astronauts to ensure a safe launch.

 SAFETY WARNINGS 

1. All instructions in the book must be carried out under adult supervision.
2. The rocket must be launched outside, in an area with no obstacles overhead. Stand at a safe distance and wear safety goggles.
3. Keep young children, pets and any unsuspecting passers-by away from the rocket launch.
4. If your rocket still hasn't launched after five minutes, ask an adult to stand near (but not right next to) the rocket and gently kick it over so the rocket is facing away from people and any fragile objects. They can then safely kick the rocket off the launcher. Never put your face over the unlaunched rocket.
5. In case of injury, seek medical advice immediately.

 ADVICE TO ASTRONAUTS

Read all the instructions before beginning and follow them carefully with adult supervision. Always close scissors after use and put lids on glue. Follow the safety instructions on the packet when using bicarbonate of soda. Be careful handling any pieces of plastic that may have sharp edges, and always put away all materials safely after use.

 A NOTE ON FIRST AID

In case of injury, always seek medical advice.

HOW TO BUILD A ROCKET

FRAN SCOTT Illustrated by PAUL BOSTON

WALKER BOOKS
AND SUBSIDIARIES
LONDON • BOSTON • SYDNEY • AUCKLAND

ABOUT ME

Oh, hey there! I'm Fran and I am going to be your building partner as you make your very own rocket. Don't worry, you are in safe hands: I build things for a living – mostly science demonstration props (big machines or structures that help explain the science behind how the world works). I've done some awesome things, such as coding exploding fireworks live onstage and building the world's largest battery made of lemons (you know the saying, "When life gives you lemons ... make a battery!").

I work with TV and radio shows, scientific institutions and engineering companies to help explain anything from electricity to genetics. I present podcasts on the latest engineering innovations. And I've also presented on CBBC and BBC Bitesize, so you may have seen my smiling face on there too.

ABOUT BUILDING THINGS

When I was your age, I loved building things (and still do), but it was not (and still isn't) easy. Building things takes a giant leap of faith. It can be scary trying something for the first time, not knowing how it's going to work out. Sometimes a model-making kit would sit in my bedroom for years as I built up the courage to try it. Do you know why? Because I was scared I'd get it wrong.

So I say to you now what I wish I'd said to myself back then: getting things "wrong" is all part of the making process. When things have gone "wrong", they've really gone right. That's because without making mistakes, we'd never learn how to get better at things – we'd never improve. As you go through this book, don't worry if things don't work out first time, or don't look fantastic straight away. I promise you, step by step we will get there ... together.

I've worked really hard to come up with a rocket design that is not only exciting to launch, but also fun to make (if sometimes a bit messy). So enjoy the process, and let's get stuck in! First step: what <u>is</u> a rocket?

SPACE ROCKET

THIS IS A SPACE ROCKET. SPACE ROCKETS ARE MADE UP OF MILLIONS OF DIFFERENT PARTS AND CAN LOOK VERY DIFFERENT DEPENDING ON THE MISSION THEY HAVE BEEN MADE FOR. GENERALLY, THOUGH, SPACE ROCKETS HAVE FOUR DIFFERENT SECTIONS:

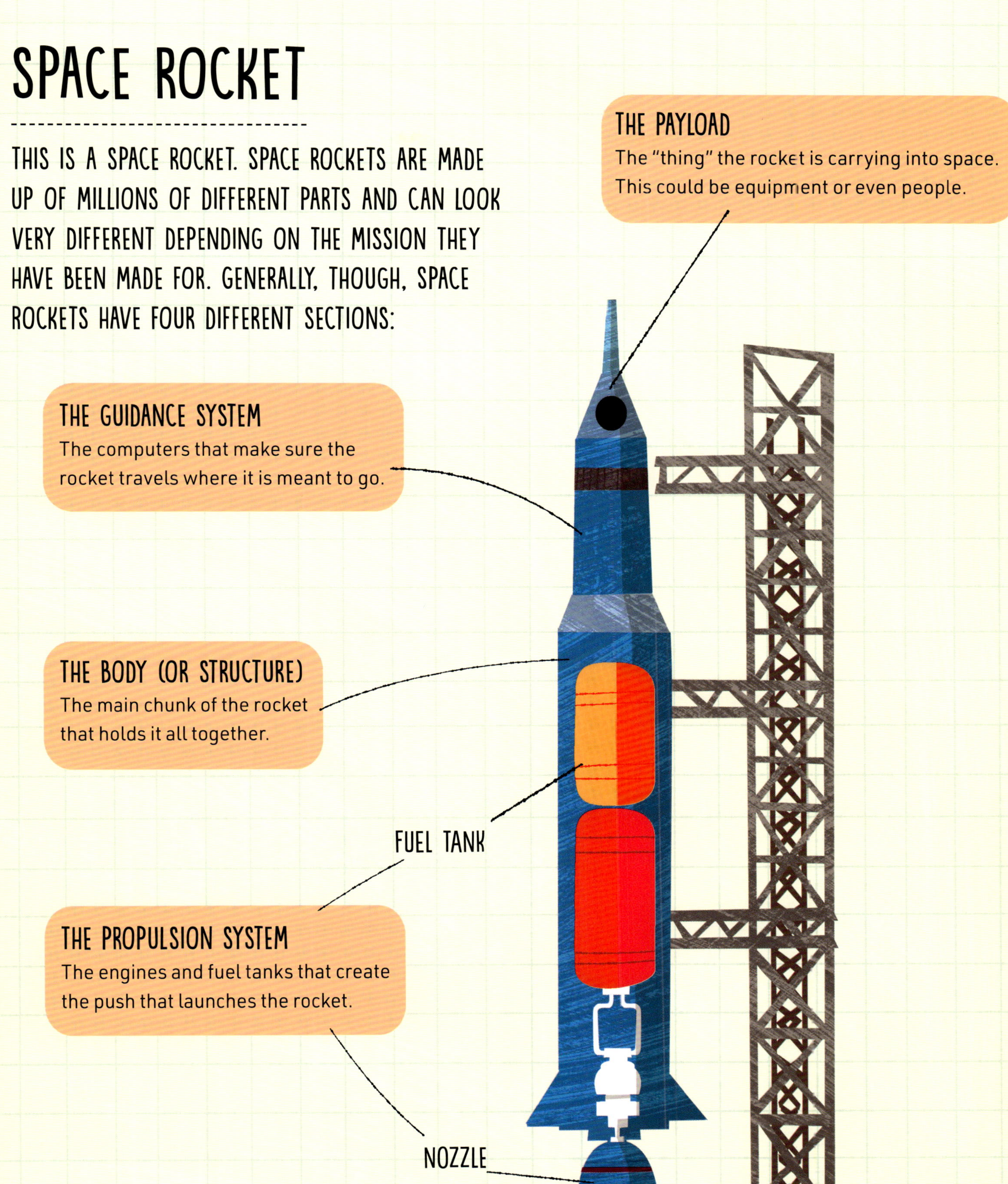

YOUR ROCKET

YOUR ROCKET WILL HAVE MOST OF THESE PARTS TOO.

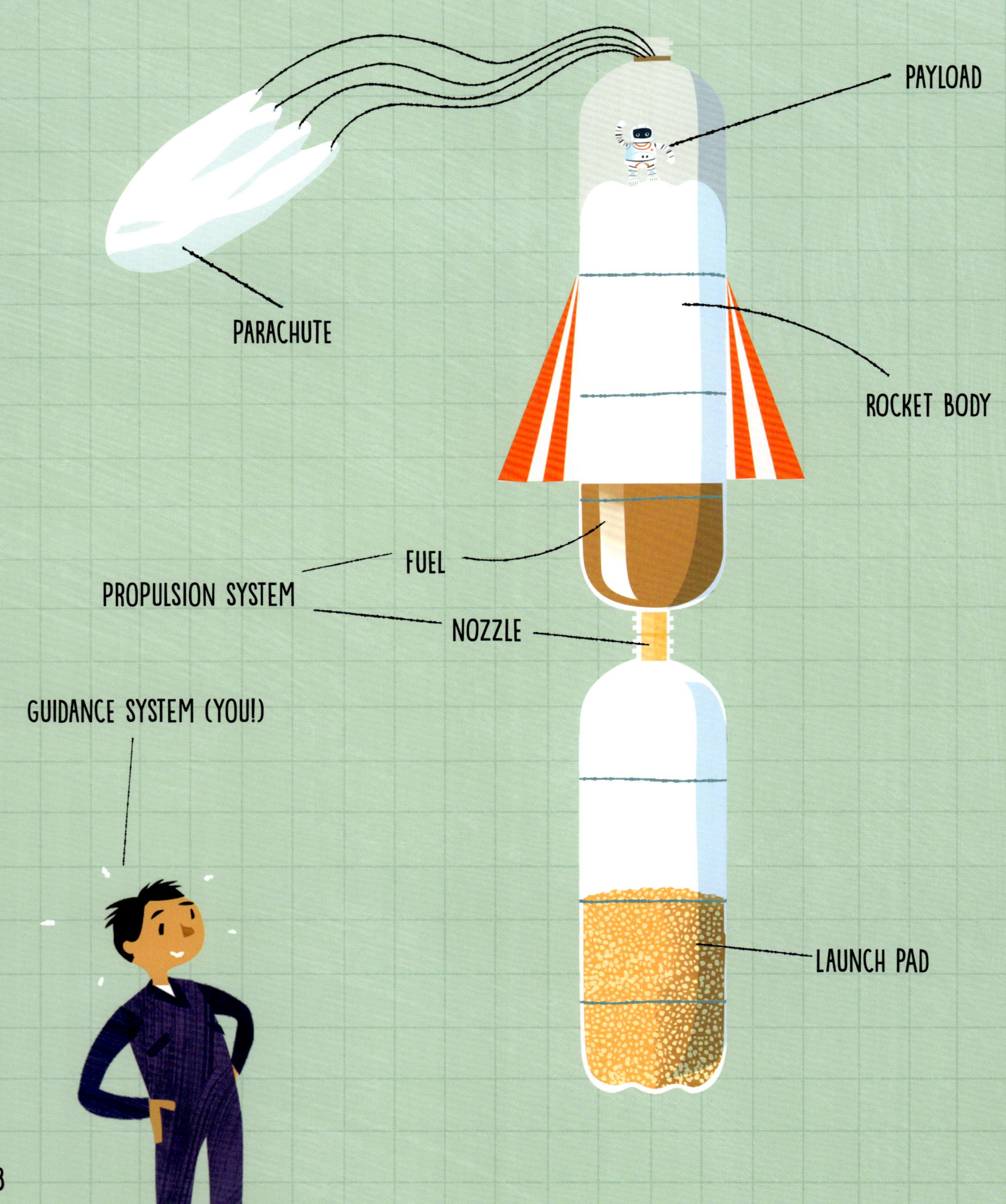

YOU WILL NEED

I'VE DESIGNED YOUR ROCKET SO THAT YOU CAN BUY MOST OF THE PARTS FROM YOUR LOCAL SUPERMARKET OR EVEN FIND THEM IN YOUR RECYCLING BIN!

- 2-litre fizzy drinks bottle (x 3)
- Ruler
- Tape measure (a cloth one is best)
- Pen
- Scissors
- PVC tape
- Tiny toy person (approx. 3 g)
- Sticky tack
- A cork
- 1 kg bag of sand (or rice, lentils, gravel)
- All-purpose glue
- Weighing scales (optional)
- Funnel (optional)
- Measuring jug
- Sharp pencil
- Vinegar (approx. 500 ml per launch)
- Bicarbonate of soda (sometimes called baking soda) (2 teaspoons per launch)
- Toilet roll
- Cotton thread
- Sticky tape
- Stopwatch
- Safety goggles

OPTIONAL EXTRAS:

- 8 cm by 12 cm sheet of thin, stiff plastic or waterproof card (x 2)
- Elastic band
- 40 cm by 40 cm square of thin plastic (such as a good quality bin bag)

YOU NOW HAVE ALL THE GEAR, BUT PROBABLY ZERO IDEA ABOUT HOW TO USE IT. WELL, MY FRIEND, DON'T YOU WORRY, BECAUSE STEP BY STEP WE'RE GOING TO MAKE THIS STUFF REACH THE STARS (WELL, ALMOST). BUT BEFORE WE DO, WE NEED TO KNOW THE SCIENCE BEHIND GETTING THINGS INTO SPACE, SO LET'S FLY OVER TO THE ROCKET ACADEMY!

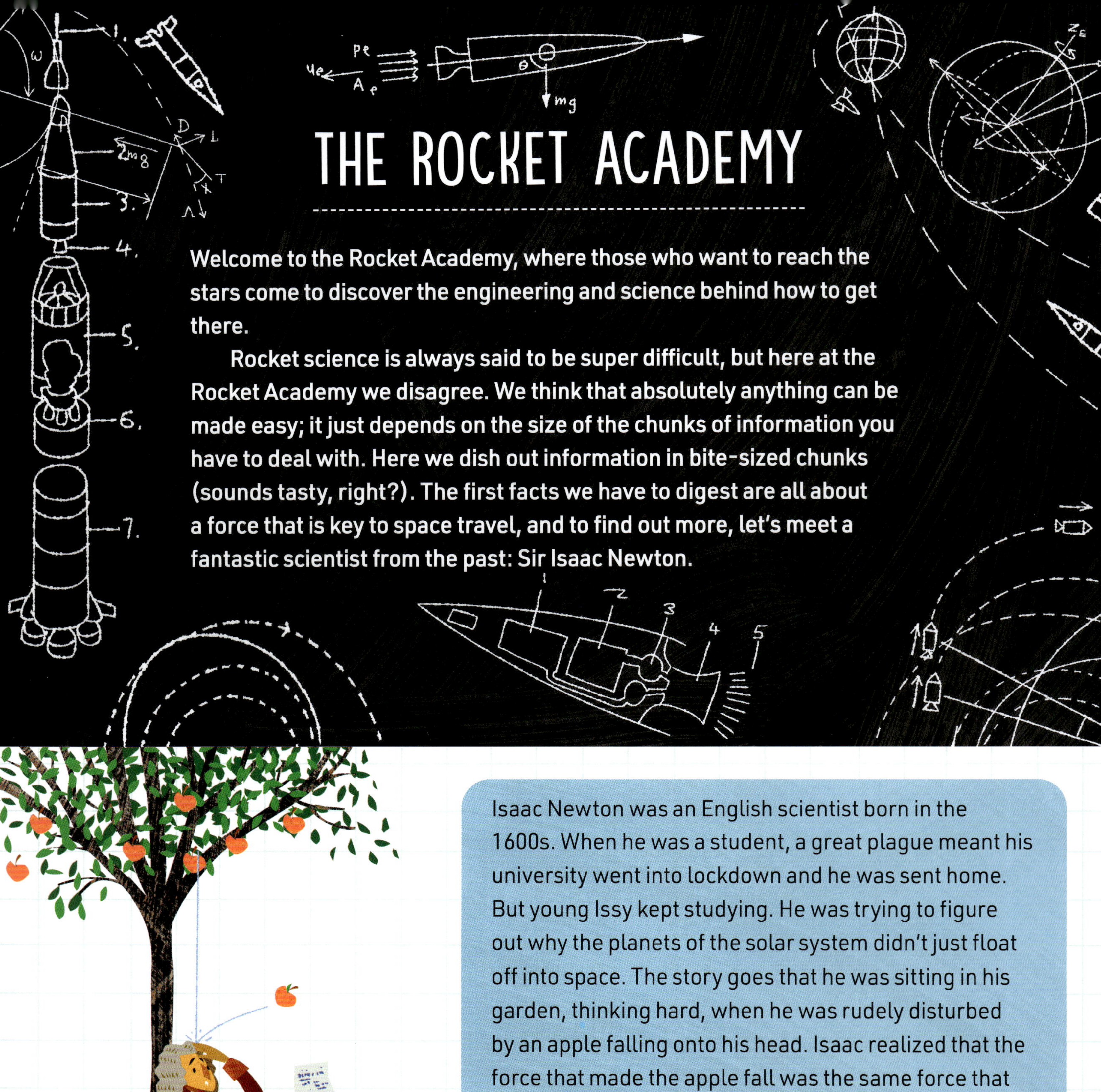

THE ROCKET ACADEMY

Welcome to the Rocket Academy, where those who want to reach the stars come to discover the engineering and science behind how to get there.

Rocket science is always said to be super difficult, but here at the Rocket Academy we disagree. We think that absolutely anything can be made easy; it just depends on the size of the chunks of information you have to deal with. Here we dish out information in bite-sized chunks (sounds tasty, right?). The first facts we have to digest are all about a force that is key to space travel, and to find out more, let's meet a fantastic scientist from the past: Sir Isaac Newton.

Isaac Newton was an English scientist born in the 1600s. When he was a student, a great plague meant his university went into lockdown and he was sent home. But young Issy kept studying. He was trying to figure out why the planets of the solar system didn't just float off into space. The story goes that he was sitting in his garden, thinking hard, when he was rudely disturbed by an apple falling onto his head. Isaac realized that the force that made the apple fall was the same force that kept the planets in their place around the Sun: GRAVITY.

But it was not all good news. Gravity causes a big problem for those of us trying to launch rockets. Luckily, solving engineering problems is what we do at the Rocket Academy.

PROBLEM: GRAVITY PULLS US DOWN

So gravity is a helpful force that stops everything just floating off. But gravity is actually much, MUCH more than that. Did you know that the heavier an object is, the more gravity it has? And also, the further away you get from an object, the weaker its gravity pull gets?

Well, this is all true (in fact it's what Isaac came up with under that tree), and it means that the annoying/interesting thing is: in order for a rocket to be launched into space and go to other planets, it needs to be able to reach a point where the Earth's gravity is weak enough that it doesn't cause the rocket to just fall straight back down to the ground. But with the Earth being as heavy as it is (it weighs 6 million, million, million, million kg ... that's a 6 followed by 24 zeros!), a rocket has A LOT of gravity to fight against.

SOLUTION

We can beat gravity by getting to grips with the "Laws of Motion". These aren't the kind of laws that could be used to arrest a rocket, but instead are laws of physics that help explain how the world works, which our pal Isaac came up with. Once we understand these laws, we can guess how objects will move and behave, and use this knowledge to get our rocket flying. So how do they work? Let's find out. Time for our next tasty chunk of information!

DID YOU KNOW?

EVERY OBJECT HAS GRAVITY, FROM APPLES TO PLANETS TO ICE CREAM. BUT THE HEAVIER SOMETHING IS, THE STRONGER ITS PULL OF GRAVITY. THIS IS WHY WHEN YOU DROP AN APPLE (OR YOUR ICE CREAM), YOU SEE IT FALLING DOWN TO THE EARTH, RATHER THAN THE EARTH BEING PULLED UP.

FIRST LAW OF MOTION

A BIT OF FORCE WOULD BE NICE.

ER... IS ANYTHING GOING TO FORCE ME TO STOP?

This law tells us that unless something is pushed or pulled by a force, then it's not going to start moving. But if an object is already moving, then without an extra force it isn't going to stop.

To be fair, this one does seem pretty obvious. Objects don't just start leaping across the room by themselves, do they? But it means that if we want our rocket to lift off, we'll need a force to get it to start moving, like giving our skater a push. We'll also need that force to be stronger than the pulling force of gravity. On a rocket this force is known as thrust, so we're going to need THRUST to get our rocket off the ground.

SECOND LAW OF MOTION

This law says that the lighter something is and the harder you push it, the more that something will speed up.

Now, to fight against the pull of Earth's gravity, we need our rocket to speed up quickly and go super fast, so we're going to need our rocket to be super LIGHT. And we're not just going to need *some* thrust, but lots and lots and *lots* of THRUST to give it this harder "push".

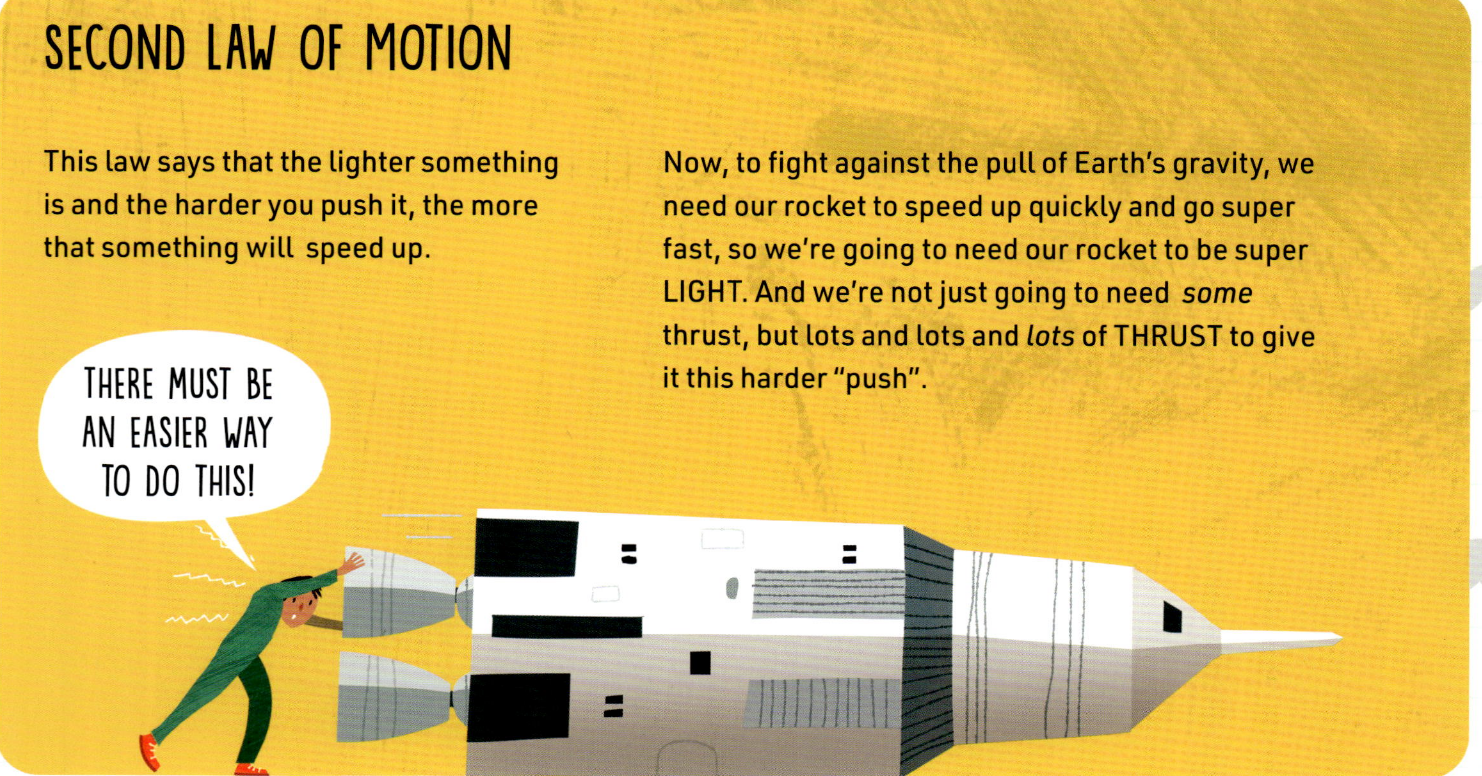

THIRD LAW OF MOTION

This law says that for something to move in one direction with a certain amount of force, then there must be a push in the opposite direction which has just as much force.

This means that for our rocket to travel upwards, this THRUST force must push DOWN towards the ground. And again, we're going to need lots of thrust – like fill-up-your-bag-then-fill-up-your-pockets-and-then-grab-a-little-bit-more-for-good-luck amount of thrust. You get the picture.

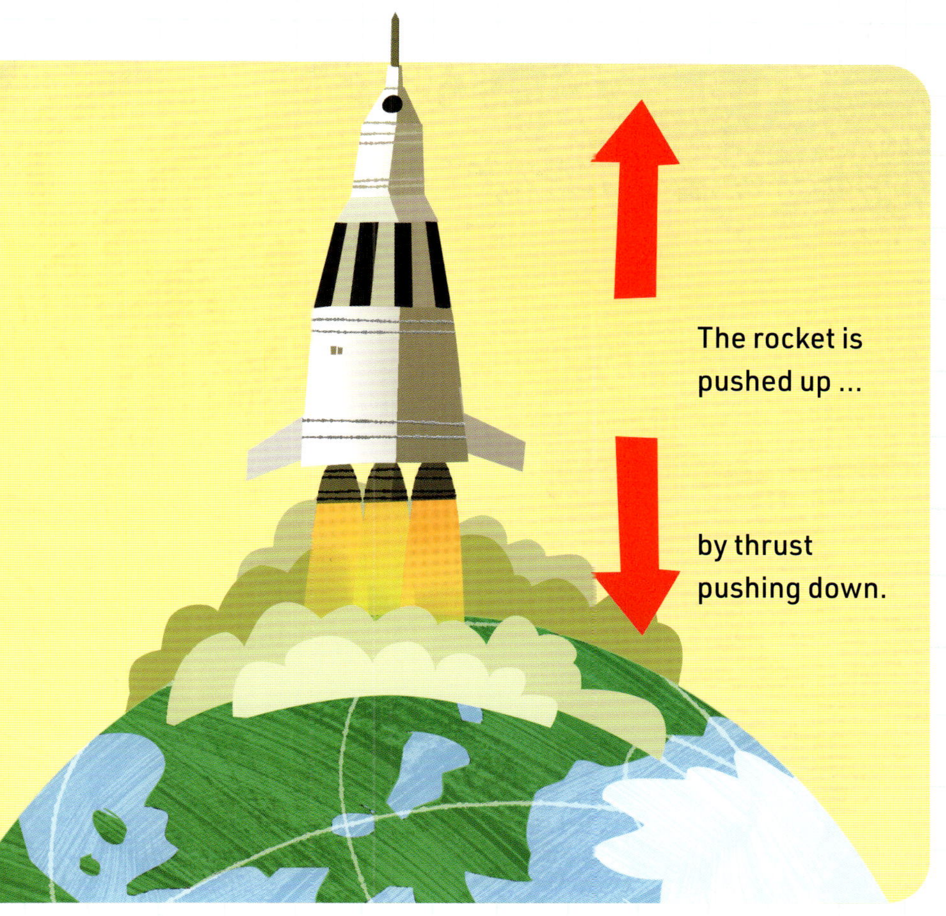

DID YOU KNOW?

IN ORDER FOR A ROCKET TO WIN THE FIGHT AGAINST EARTH'S GRAVITY AND FLY TO OTHER PLANETS OR THE MOON, IT NEEDS TO REACH A PANT-RIPPING 40,000 KPH. THAT'S MORE THAN 100 TIMES FASTER THAN A FORMULA ONE CAR!

WHAT NEXT?

AND THERE WE HAVE IT, A BITE-SIZED ROCKET SCIENCE MEAL, SHOWING US THAT IN ORDER TO OVERCOME THE FORCE OF GRAVITY AND LAUNCH SUCCESSFULLY, YOUR ROCKET WILL NEED TO BE LIGHT, HAVE LOTS OF THRUST, AND YOU'LL NEED TO MAKE SURE THAT THRUST IS PUSHING DOWN TOWARDS THE GROUND.

YOU MUST NOW BE FULL OF SCIENCE. THAT SAID, THERE'S NOT MUCH TIME TO PUT YOUR FEET UP AND FALL ASLEEP ON THE SOFA BECAUSE (DRUM ROLL PLEASE ...) YOU HAVE JUST GRADUATED FROM THE ROCKET ACADEMY. AND THAT MEANS TWO THINGS:

1. YOU CAN BOW TO YOUR FANS AS YOU RECEIVE APPLAUSE!
2. YOU'RE NOW PART OF THE TEAM BEHIND A ROCKET LAUNCH!

TURN THE PAGE TO MEET YOUR TEAMMATES...

MEET THE TEAM

THERE ARE LOADS OF PEOPLE WHO WORK ON ROCKETS, WITH LOTS OF DIFFERENT SKILLS, TO MAKE A MISSION SUCCESSFUL. HERE ARE JUST A FEW OF THEM!

You've probably heard of my job. In space, I do scientific experiments and fix equipment. There are astronauts from lots of different countries; we all know at least two languages so we can talk to each other when we're on a mission together.

I build the rocket and all the different parts it uses. I work in a special "cleanroom" to keep the spacecraft as clean as possible. I'm part of a team of specialists who work with the engineers to build, test and improve the rocket.

SPACECRAFT TECHNICIAN

Propulsion is another word for thrust, so it's my job to design how the engines make the thrust for the rocket. This not only gets the rocket into space, but also steers it once it's there.

I work with all of the teams and look at the project as a whole. I make sure all the different parts will work together.

I think about the shape and strength of the rocket. I make sure we use the right materials in the right way so that the rocket can cope with the huge forces it faces during take-off, as well as the weird conditions that are found in space.

Some missions are too dangerous or long for astronauts. These need onboard computers, and sometimes even robots instead. I design robots that can collect samples, take measurements and move around on command. Computers also need to be coded with software to run by themselves.

Sending objects into space is all well and good, but we need to keep track of where they are and what they're doing. I design machines to communicate with the astronauts or the computers on board.

I lead a team of flight controllers. We are in the control room making sure a mission is completed safely. We look after the launch and monitor the spacecraft throughout the entire mission. We work in shifts so we can watch the spacecraft all the time and fix problems as soon as they happen.

AND THE NEWEST TEAM MEMBER IS, OF COURSE, YOU! SO LET'S HEAD TO MISSION CONTROL AND DISCOVER HOW TO BUILD A ROCKET!

CHAPTER ONE

THE ROCKET BODY

YOU LOOK AROUND. THERE ARE MASSIVE SCREENS ON THE WALL AND ROWS AND ROWS OF COMPUTERS, EACH WITH ITS VERY OWN HEADSET-WEARING OPERATOR. OPERATORS WHO ALL TURN AND LOOK AT YOU WHEN YOUR TRAINERS ACCIDENTALLY MAKE THAT FUNNY SQUEAKING NOISE ON THE FLOOR. THEY SMILE AT YOU. THEY LOOK FRIENDLY. "HAVE YOU SEEN IT YET?" ONE OF THEM ASKS, GESTURING TO THE LARGE WINDOW TO YOUR LEFT. YOU PRESS YOUR NOSE RIGHT UP AGAINST THE GLASS AND CRANK YOUR NECK UPWARDS TO SEE ALL OF IT. NOW, THAT IS A ROCKET. THE OPERATOR CONTINUES, "YOU MUST BE OUR NEWEST RECRUIT FROM THE ROCKET ACADEMY. WELCOME TO MISSION CONTROL!"

EXCITEDLY, YOU PICK UP YOUR SPANNERS, SPACESUIT AND SANDWICHES (STILL HUNGRY?). THE SKY IS THE LIMIT. YOUR JOB AT MISSION CONTROL IS TO BUILD A ROCKET JUST AS GLORIOUS AS THAT ONE OUTSIDE, AND YOU CAN'T WAIT TO GET STARTED. GO ON THEN, READ ON...

TASK ONE: BUILD THE BODY OF THE ROCKET

Sometimes getting started is the hardest bit, so we're going to begin by building the most obvious part of the rocket, and that is the rocket body. The body is the big bit that gives the rocket its shape. It also provides a structure to store the objects that are going to travel to space (called the payload) and a place to store the fuel that the rocket needs to fly.

Building the body of the rocket is like riding a pogo stick while trying to eat spaghetti. You have to think about doing a few very different jobs at the same time, and as we know (from the spaghetti on your shoes), that is not always easy.

So, let's take a closer look at what these jobs are and find a solution that lets us do them all at the same time.

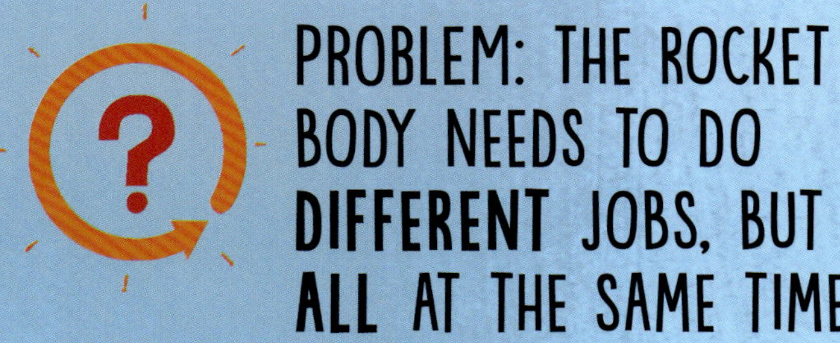

PROBLEM: THE ROCKET BODY NEEDS TO DO **DIFFERENT** JOBS, BUT **ALL** AT THE SAME TIME

The jobs the rocket body needs to do are:

JOB 1 Provide an overall structure for the rocket (so that it doesn't flop like a week old balloon)

JOB 2 Provide a way to launch the rocket

JOB 3 Provide a way to carry the payload into space

Coming up with a way to do each of these jobs on its own isn't actually that difficult, but tackling ALL of them at the SAME time is like playing rocket-shaped whack-a-mole. Just as you solve one problem, your solution will somehow cause a new problem to pop up from nowhere. Take a look at what I mean...

TO MAKE A ROCKET STRONG, IT MAKES SENSE TO BUILD IT OUT OF METAL ...

BUT METAL IS HEAVY ...

AND NEWTON'S SECOND LAW OF MOTION SAYS THAT FOR A ROCKET TO LAUNCH IT NEEDS TO BE AS LIGHT AS POSSIBLE ...

THIS MEANS WE SHOULD MAKE THE ROCKET AS SMALL AS POSSIBLE BECAUSE LESS METAL MEANS A LIGHTER ROCKET ...

BUT NEWTON'S SECOND AND THIRD LAWS OF MOTION SAY THAT FOR AN OBJECT TO TRAVEL FAST IT NEEDS A BIG THRUST. A BIG THRUST MEANS LOTS OF FUEL – SO THE ROCKET NEEDS TO BE BIG TO CARRY ENOUGH FUEL.

Complicated, right? And that's not all. When space rockets launch, what comes out the bottom of them? No, not that! It's ... fire. (Well, fire and gas.) And fire is hot. And if you are using your rocket to carry important things into space – like satellites or maybe even your Auntie Gill – you don't want those objects to be toasted.

All this means the body of the rocket needs to be STRONG, LIGHT and BIG, with the payload well away from the launch end of the rocket. Yes, that is a long list and it will need a clever solution, but that's why they call it rocket science and call you a rocket scientist.

DID YOU KNOW?

THE ROCKETS THAT SENT ASTRONAUTS TO THE MOON WERE 110 METRES HIGH. THAT'S TALLER THAN THE STATUE OF LIBERTY (WHICH HAS NOT GONE TO THE MOON).

SOLUTION

The way to solve most of these problems is with the material the rocket body is made from. And the material rocket scientists tend to choose is either titanium or aluminium. These are strong but light metals. Engineers also design rockets so the payload is at the top and the launch end is at the bottom. Tick, tick, tick – problems solved.

But rest your rockets for a moment, as you're not going to build YOUR rocket out of titanium. Oh no, I promised you that your rocket could be built with items from the supermarket – and good luck finding titanium in the milk aisle! We're not just going to copy what other engineers do; we are going to use something different. But what can you use that is STRONG, LIGHT and BIG?

Well, gather round. Here's the moment you've all been waiting for (well, at least for the last 30 seconds)... The winner of "The-Best-Supermarket-Object-to-Build-a-Rocket-Body-So-It's-Strong-Light-and-Big-Could-This-Name-Be-Any-Longer" award is ... a fizzy drinks bottle.

Yes, a 2-litre plastic bottle is perfect. Of course, you'll need to do a bit of building to convert this cola container so it's more *at* home with the sparkling stars than *a* home for sparkling drinks. So let's have a look at how to do just that...

ASK AN ADULT TO HELP

THE ROCKET BODY

WHAT YOU'LL NEED

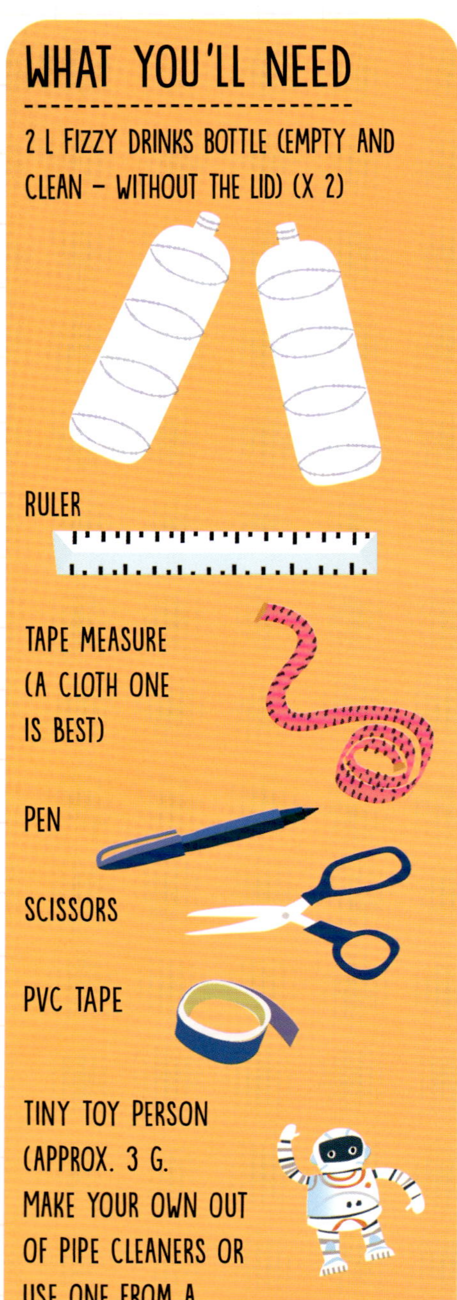

1. Take one of the bottles and push the cork about 2 cm into its opening (do not push it all the way into the bottle!). Check that it fits tightly – try both ends of the cork. If the cork is too small, wrap PVC tape around it a few times.

TOP TIP

YOU CAN CHECK YOUR CORK IS TIGHT BY ADDING SOME WATER TO THE BOTTLE, PUTTING IN THE CORK AND TURNING THE BOTTLE UPSIDE DOWN OVER A SINK. IF THE BOTTLE DOESN'T LEAK, THE CORK FITS.

2. Once your cork is about 2 cm in and nice and straight, draw a line around it at the point it meets the bottle so you know how far to push it in next time.

3 Take the other bottle and stand it on a table. Measure 15 cm up from the table and draw a line all the way around the bottle at this point. Underneath this line draw an "X".

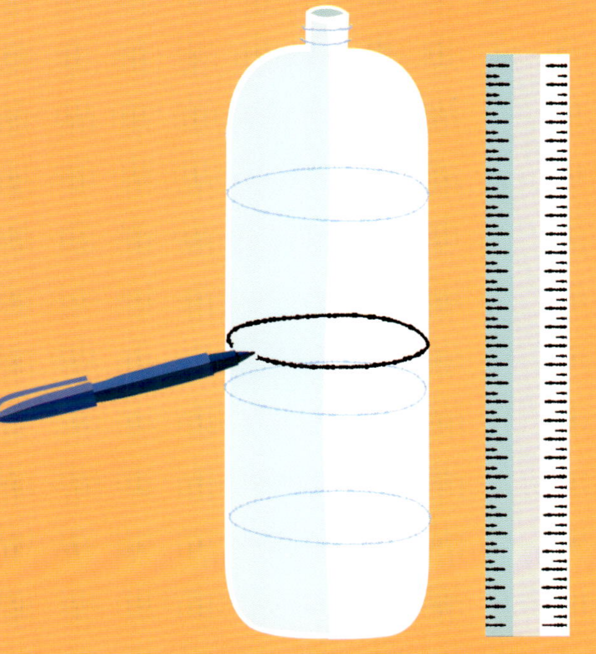

4 Now measure 22 cm up from the table and draw another line all the way around the bottle.

5 With an adult's help, cut the lower section off at the 15 cm mark. Put the bottom section of the bottle (the one with the "X" on) into the recycling and keep the top section. This is going to be your space capsule, where the payload (your tiny toy person) will sit.

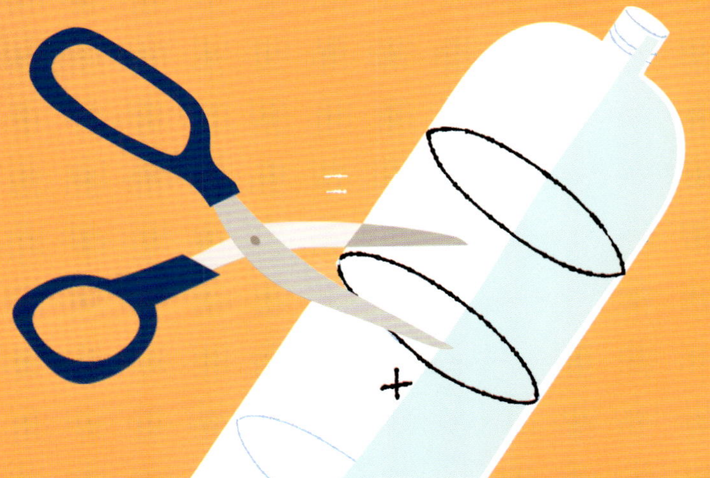

REMEMBER: YOU NEED AN ADULT TO HELP YOU!

6 Take your space capsule and wrap the tape measure around the line you drew in Step 4.

Keeping the tape measure tight, make marks at 1 cm, 3 cm, 9 cm, 11 cm, 17 cm, 19 cm, 25 cm and 27 cm. Stick the tape measure to the bottle, if that makes it easier.

7 Using a ruler, draw straight lines down from these marks to the bottom edge of the bottle. Don't worry, these lines don't have to be super straight.

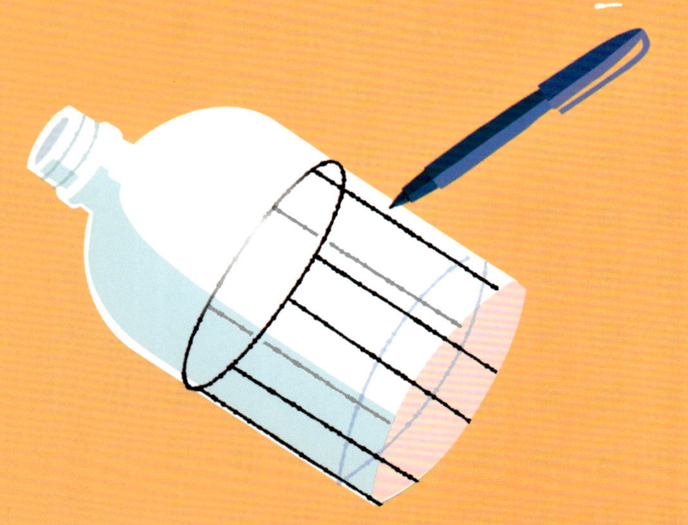

8 With an adult's help, cut along each of these lines, to make four thick flaps (about 6 cm wide) and four thinner flaps (about 2 cm wide).

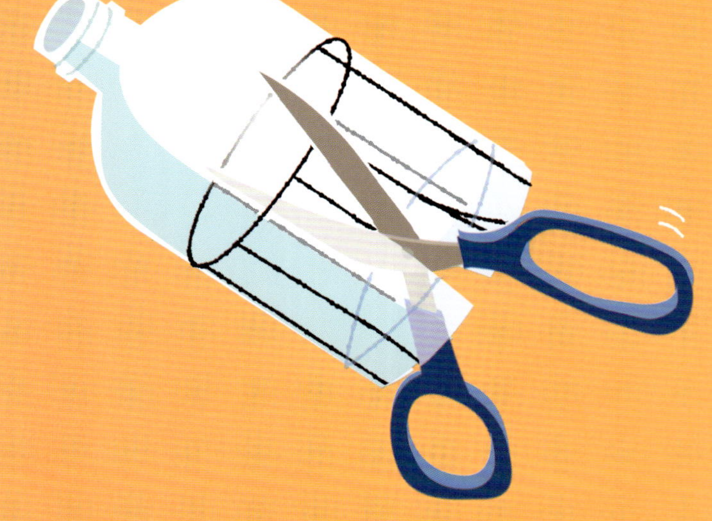

9 Cut off the four thick flaps so you now have gaps that are about 6 cm wide. The flaps can be put into the recycling.

10 Now take your tiny toy person and position it in your space capsule. Stick it on the inside of the bottle, near the bottle opening, using the sticky tack.

11 Finally, take the first bottle (the one with the cork in), hold it upside down and place the space capsule onto the base of the bottle, like it's a hat. The capsule should stay in place when the bottle is held straight, but fall off when the bottle is tilted. Perfect!

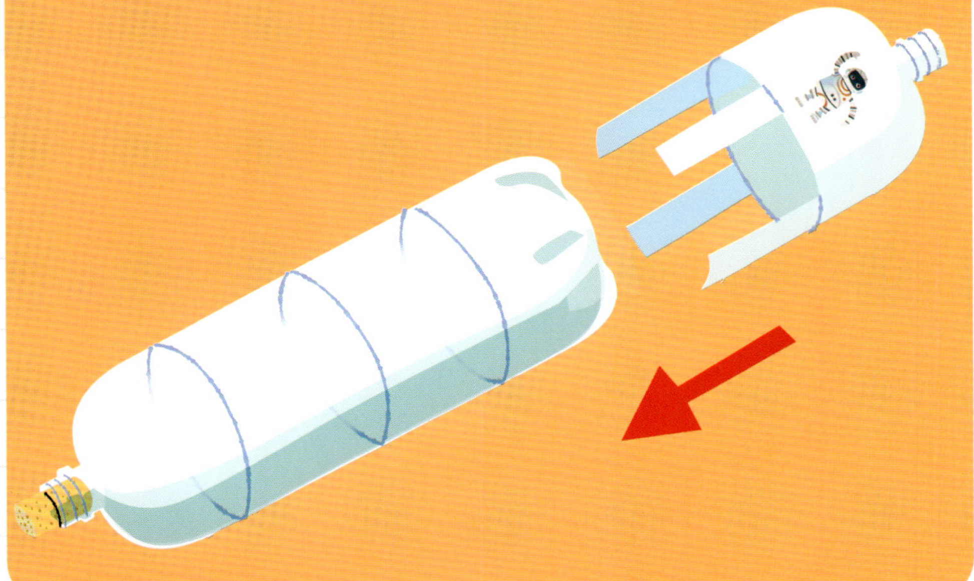

AWESOME!

THAT'S IT – YOU'VE MADE THE ROCKET BODY, BUT YOU NOW WANT (SOME MIGHT SAY NEED) YOUR ROCKET TO ACTUALLY GO SOMEWHERE. AND FOR THAT, YOU'LL NEED A LAUNCH PAD...

SO, ENGINEER, FLY YOURSELF OVER TO CHAPTER TWO TO MAKE YOUR ROCKET DREAMS COME TRUE.

CHAPTER TWO

THE LAUNCH PAD

FOR A ROCKET TO "ROCKET" INTO SPACE IT NEEDS A LAUNCH PAD. LAUNCH PADS DO LOTS OF JOBS – THEY PROVIDE A WAY FOR THE FUEL TO BE LOADED, A WAY TO INSPECT THE ROCKET BEFORE TAKE-OFF, AND THEY EVEN HAVE A WALKWAY TO ALLOW THE CREW TO ENTER THE ROCKET! BUT MOST IMPORTANTLY, A LAUNCH PAD HOLDS THE ROCKET IN PLACE AND MAKES SURE IT STAYS THE RIGHT WAY UP.

TASK TWO: BUILD THE LAUNCH PAD

When it comes to your launch pad, you don't need one quite that fancy because your fuel and astronaut will already be on board. But you DO need to build a launch pad to ... well ... launch your rocket. And also – very importantly – to hold your rocket in place during the countdown.

But which way is the right way up? Well, for your rocket to launch UPWARDS the thrust must push DOWN into the ground. Look back at page 13, and you'll see this is Newton's Third Law of Motion. But making the thrust push down gives us another problem...

PROBLEM: LET'S PLAY OPPOSITES

So, for a rocket to fly UPWARDS, the thrust from the fuel needs to push DOWN. But with your rocket body, the force will come from the bottle opening, which is at the TOP of the bottle. This means that for your rocket to fly, the bottle will need to be upside down, with the opening at the bottom. But (or, as we're talking about the rocket's bottom, should I say butt?) if you try to balance the bottle on its opening, it's going to fall over like a one-legged giraffe. So the *bottom* line is that we need some support to hold the rocket in place, and make sure that its top is at the bottom. Top stuff!

SOLUTION

The solution to all of this is to build a launch pad that has two key features. It needs to be:

1. **STABLE** – so neither it nor the rocket falls over at launch time. (Not to be confused with lunchtime – though both are great times of the day.)
2. **WATERPROOF** – so it doesn't matter if it gets wet from rocket fuel (which we will add later).

After testing lots and lots of different materials, the team at mission control found the absolutely one-of-a-kind, perfect material to build the launch pad. And – you'll never believe this – it's another 2-litre plastic drinks bottle! Well, this is one way to recycle them, I suppose!

ASK AN ADULT TO HELP

THE LAUNCH PAD

WHAT YOU'LL NEED

YOUR ROCKET BODY (WITH CORK)

2 L FIZZY DRINKS BOTTLE (EMPTY AND CLEAN, WITHOUT THE LID)

1 KG BAG OF SAND (OR RICE, LENTILS, GRAVEL)

PVC TAPE

ALL-PURPOSE GLUE

WEIGHING SCALES (OPTIONAL)

FUNNEL (OPTIONAL)

1. Fill up the new bottle with sand until it weighs approximately 1 kg. You can use a funnel to help you if you need. (I did!)

TOP TIP

IF YOU DON'T HAVE ANY KITCHEN SCALES, JUST POUR UNTIL THE BOTTLE IS MORE THAN HALF FULL.

2. Remove the cork from the rocket body and insert the opposite end into the top of the new bottle. Again, wrap PVC tape around the cork if it is too small to form a tight seal.

3 Stick the cork firmly in place with the glue, making sure that the glue doesn't go past the line you drew earlier. Leave the glue to dry.

AWESOME!

ROCKET BODY? CHECK!
LAUNCH PAD? CHECK!
WAY TO FUEL YOUR ROCKET SO THAT IT FLIES INTO SPACE AND MAKES YOU A WORLD-FAMOUS ENGINEER? AH ... THAT, MY FRIEND, IS ALL IN CHAPTER THREE.*

*OK, MAYBE NOT THE WORLD-FAMOUS ENGINEER PART... THAT'S IN CHAPTER SEVEN OF COURSE.

TOP TIP

IF YOU DON'T HAVE TIME FOR THE GLUE TO DRY, USE TAPE INSTEAD TO STICK THE CORK TIGHTLY IN PLACE.

THE FUEL

OVER THE YEARS ROCKETS HAVE USED LOTS OF DIFFERENT KINDS OF FUEL, FROM GUNPOWDER BACK IN THE 1200S TO THE KEROSENE (SUPER-CHARGED PETROL) OR LIQUID HYDROGEN THAT MAKE MODERN ROCKETS SHOOT OFF THIS EARTH. BUT HOW DO THESE FUELS ACTUALLY POWER A ROCKET? IT'S ALL ABOUT GETTING A REACTION...

TASK THREE: FIND YOUR FUEL

Choosing your rocket fuel can be as difficult as deciding on a flavour at an ice-cream shop – there are so many options! However, whichever fuel you use, the one thing it must do is produce enough thrust downwards to shoot your rocket upwards. To do this, the fuel needs to go through a chemical reaction.

A chemical reaction is what happens when a substance is changed into a new, different substance. Chemical reactions are hugely helpful in engineering and there are lots of different kinds. Burning is one kind, and it is what is usually done with rocket fuel. As the fuel burns, it makes lots of gas, quickly. Gas can push on things, and when you have lots of gas, you have lots of push. This gas pushes down out through the nozzle of the rocket, launching the rocket up. But for us it's not so simple. Why is it never simple?!

DID YOU KNOW?

MOST OF A ROCKET'S WEIGHT IS FUEL. FOR EVERY 10 KG OF WEIGHT, ABOUT 9 KG IS FUEL. THIS MEANS THAT WHEN THIS HUGE WEIGHT OF FUEL REACTS, IT MAKES A MASSIVE AMOUNT OF GAS, GIVING ENOUGH THRUST TO PUSH THE ROCKET UP.

PROBLEM: FUEL IS HOT STUFF

We need a chemical reaction to make the gas, to give us push down, to launch the rocket up.

But however sensible you pretend to be, I can't let you play with fire and go around burning rocket fuel. Also, if we burned fuel in your rocket, then it would end up as melted as a cheese toastie (but not half as tasty). This means we need to skip the burning part completely and instead come up with a different way to make gas. A lot of gas. Quickly. Any ideas? No smirking allowed.

SOLUTION

We can do this through a chemical reaction that ISN'T burning, called "neutralization". This reaction involves mixing together an acid and an alkali (pronounced *al-kar-lie*). I get that acids and alkalis sound like something you'd only be able to find in a chemistry lab, but believe it or not, you can also find them in your local supermarket – just like I promised. We are going to use some of these supermarket acids and alkalis to make your very own rocket fuel.

HOW TO MAKE ROCKET FUEL

Before you mix acids and alkalis together, it's good to know what you're doing, so here is your quick chemistry cookbook. I've called it a cookbook because so many acids and alkalis can be found in the kitchen. This includes the ones you're going to use for your rocket fuel, which are vinegar (acid) and bicarbonate of soda (alkali).

The reason acids and alkalis are useful to us is because of how they react. Here's an example of what happens when you mix them together:

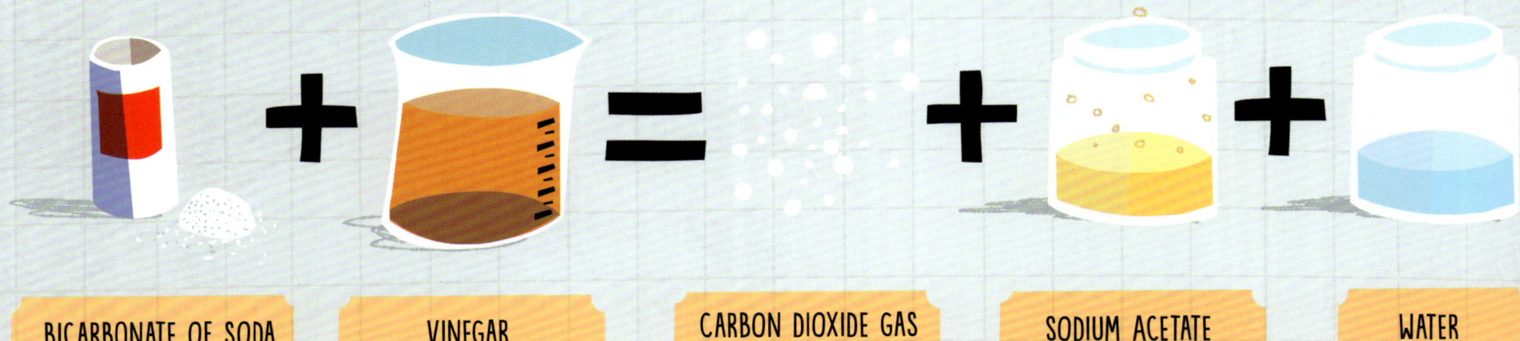

BICARBONATE OF SODA + VINEGAR = CARBON DIOXIDE GAS + SODIUM ACETATE + WATER

DID YOU KNOW?
BICARBONATE OF SODA IS USED A LOT IN BAKING AND IS SOMETIMES CALLED SODIUM BICARBONATE.

When you make your rocket fuel, you'll notice a LOT of fizzing. This is the reaction in action. It's a lot of gas being made – a gas called carbon dioxide.

It is this gas that will help launch your rocket. You see, if you trapped this gas in your rocket, then the rocket would explode – which is not great. But if you ALMOST trap it, and let it escape out of a small hole at the bottom of the rocket, the push of the gas will give you the thrust needed to launch your rocket.

But it would be a messy old launch if this reaction happened straight away. You need time to get your rocket in position – and to get out of the way! – before the gas is made. So, we're going to delay the reaction by wrapping the bicarbonate of soda in toilet paper, which the vinegar will take time to soak through. And this will make sure the launching rocket doesn't soak you!

ASK AN ADULT TO HELP

THE ROCKET FUEL

WHAT YOU'LL NEED

YOUR ROCKET BODY

MEASURING JUG

SHARP PENCIL

AND FOR EACH LAUNCH:

APPROX. 500 ML OF VINEGAR (THE CHEAPEST KIND IS FINE)

2 TEASPOONS (APPROX. 20 G) OF BICARBONATE OF SODA

3 SHEETS OF TOILET PAPER

60 CM OF COTTON THREAD

10 CM STRIPS OF STICKY TAPE (X 3)

1. Lay your strip of toilet paper flat on a table.

2. Spoon 2 teaspoons of bicarbonate of soda onto the middle sheet, in a straight-ish line, near the bottom edge.

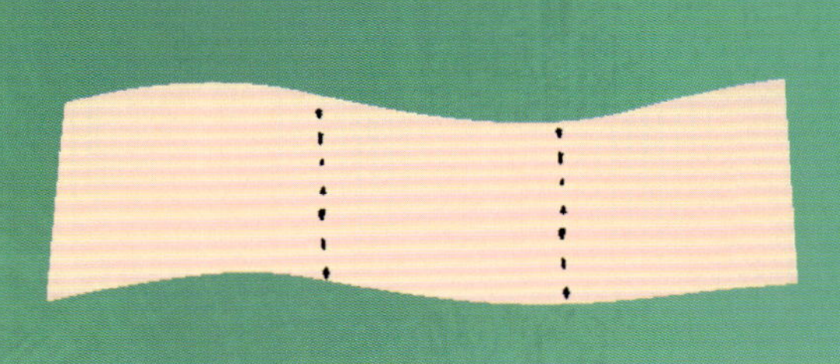

3. Fold in each of the outer sheets so they lie on top of the bicarbonate of soda.

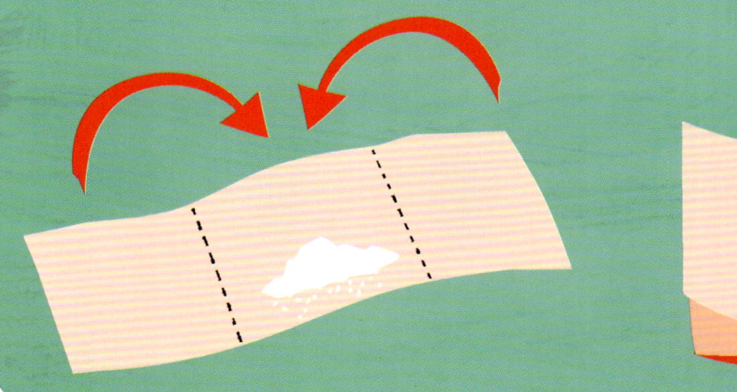

4 Now, starting from the bottom edge, tightly roll the bicarb-tissue sandwich into a sausage shape.

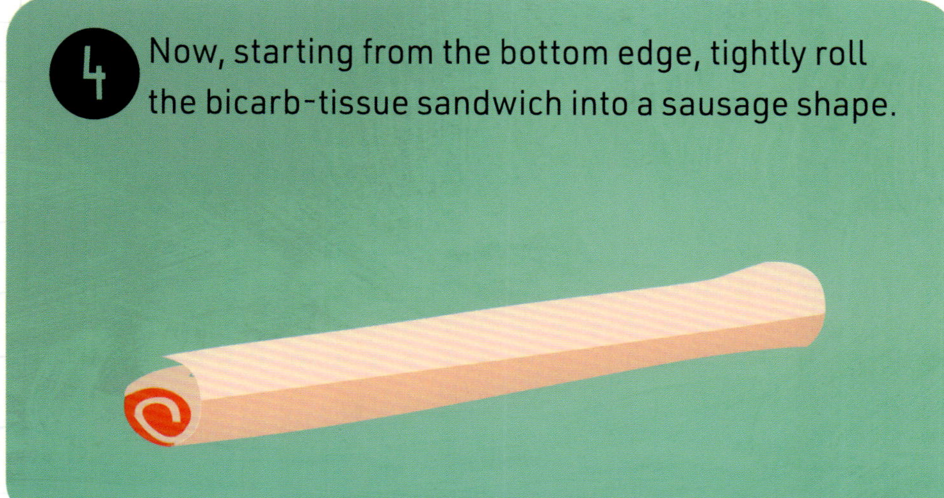

TOP TIP

THIS IS NOT EASY. YOU NEED TO MAKE SURE THAT THE BICARBONATE OF SODA DOESN'T ESCAPE AND THE TOILET PAPER DOESN'T RIP. ROLL IT SLOWLY AND CAREFULLY.

5 Once you have your tissue sausage, take two pieces of sticky tape (each about 10 cm long) and wrap them around the top and bottom of the sausage to stop it unravelling.

TOP TIP

ROLL THE TISSUE TIGHTLY ENOUGH SO THAT IT WILL FIT THROUGH THE OPENING OF THE ROCKET BODY BOTTLE.

6 Use the pencil to make six holes in the tissue between these two bits of tape – three on each side of the sausage.

CAN I SMELL SAUSAGES?

7 Take the thread and tie one end of it tightly next to one of the strips of tape on your sausage. Secure the thread in place using another strip of tape.

8 Ensure the thread is secure enough for you to hold it and lift the tissue sausage.

9 Remove the space capsule from your rocket body and turn the body around so the opening is at the top. Ensure that your tissue sausage is thin enough to fit through the opening of the bottle (but don't let it fall in ... just yet). If it doesn't fit, repeat Steps 1–8 but make sure your tissue sausage is wrapped tighter.

TOP TIP

WHEN YOU LAUNCH YOUR ROCKET, THE OPENING WILL BE AT THE BOTTOM, BUT UNTIL THEN KEEP IT AT THE TOP.

10 Measure out 500 ml of vinegar into your jug.

AWESOME!

YOU HAVE SOURCED FROM THE SUPERMARKET, RUMMAGED IN YOUR RECYCLING AND CLEARED OUT YOUR KITCHEN CUPBOARDS – YOU NOW HAVE ALL THE INGREDIENTS FOR THE PERFECT ROCKET LAUNCH. SO GATHER UP YOUR KIT, GRAB YOUR GROWN-UP AND PUT ON YOUR BIG PERSON PANTS, BECAUSE IT'S TIME FOR BLAST-OFF!

LAUNCH TIME!

OH GOOD, I'M STARVING – I HOPE IT'S SAUSAGES.

CHAPTER FOUR

COUNTDOWN TO LAUNCH

THE DAY IS HERE; THE CROWDS HAVE GATHERED. YOU HAVE BEEN WORKING TOWARDS THIS MOMENT FOR YEARS... OK, MAYBE DAYS. HOURS. WHATEVER YOUR TIME SPENT, MY FRIENDS, ALL YOUR HARD WORK HAS BEEN WORTH IT. YOUR ROCKET IS COMPLETE, THE LAUNCH PAD HAS BEEN CONSTRUCTED, THE FUEL CALCULATIONS HAVE BEEN MADE, AND YOU ARE NOW READY FOR YOUR FIRST-EVER ROCKET LAUNCH.

LET THE COUNTDOWN BEGIN...

5 You can feel the excitement in your stomach...

4 Or maybe that's just your breakfast...

3 You think back on all the hard work that brought you here...

2 The crowd all look at you, ready for you to do your thing...

1 What do you mean, you don't know what to do?

Ah, of course. I haven't actually shared with you how to do the launch yet. My bad. Stop, stop, stop! We'll be back in a second.

Before you can have the launch of your lifetime, you need the step-by-step guide to how to do it. But where on earth are we going to find that? Ummm, I wonder...

ASK AN ADULT TO HELP

THE LAUNCH

SAFETY NOTE

The rocket must be launched outside with no obstacles overhead. Stand at a safe distance and wear goggles. Keep young children, pets and passers-by away from the launch. If the rocket fails to launch, do not approach it.

1. Take all of your equipment outside – it's best to launch when it's not too windy. Find a piece of flat ground without anything hanging over it, like trees, a powerline or a roof. Put your goggles on so you are ready for action.

2. Remove the space capsule from the rocket body. Carefully pour all the vinegar into the rocket body.

3 Take your tissue sausage and carefully squeeze it into the rocket body, holding on to the thread. Don't let the tissue rip and don't let the sausage touch the vinegar.

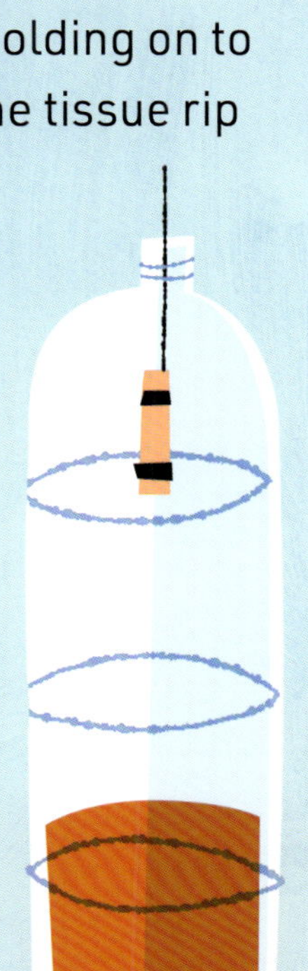

TOP TIP

IF THERE IS TOO MUCH WIND, THEN THE ROCKET MAY BLOW OVER. THE WAY TO SOLVE THIS IS TO MAKE A RING OUT OF FULL FOOD CANS AND PLACE THE LAUNCH PAD IN THE MIDDLE OF THEM.

4 Once the tissue sausage is well inside the bottle (but not touching the vinegar), stick the loose thread onto the outside of the bottle. It should hold the sausage in place and stop it falling even after you let go of the thread.

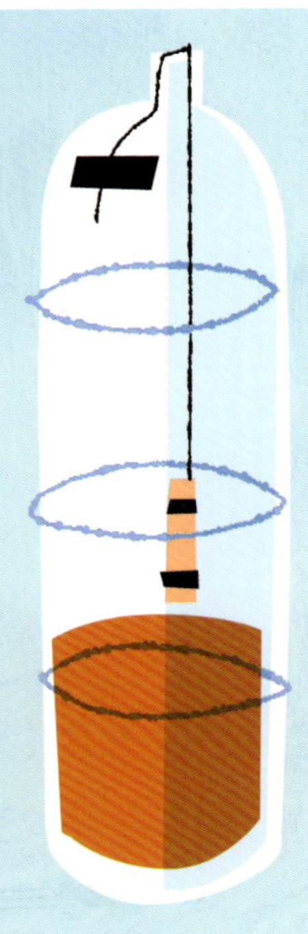

5 Now take your launch pad and put the end of the cork into the opening of your rocket body. Try to get the cork in as far as the line you drew earlier and keep it as straight as possible.

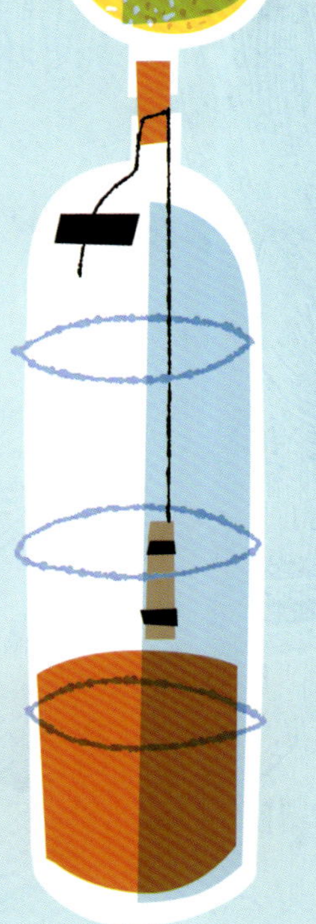

6 When you're ready for launch, turn the whole rocket-and-launch-pad combo the right way up, with the launch pad at the bottom. Holding the middle section with one hand, give the whole thing a really hard shake for three seconds.

7 Stand it on the ground with the launch pad at the bottom. Gently place the space capsule on the top of the rocket and then STAND BACK at least 2 m. Start your stopwatch.

8 There will be some fizzing, and then after about 1–2 minutes your rocket should launch into the air. Your space capsule should separate from your rocket body mid-flight.

SAFETY NOTE

If your rocket still hasn't launched after five minutes (use a timer, as five minutes is longer than you think!), this means you didn't shake it hard enough. Get an adult to go near (but not right next to) the rocket and gently kick it over so the rocket is facing away from people and any fragile objects. They can then safely kick the rocket off the launcher. Never put your face over the unlaunched rocket.

9 Try to catch the space capsule on its way back down to the ground.

WHAT'S NEXT?

Scream in delight as you see your career in space engineering take off before your eyes. Congratulations! You have launched your very own rocket. And, yes... It. Was. AWESOME! But do you know what space engineers do?

Yes, they celebrate by waving their arms in the air and shouting "Yippee". But then they try to figure out how to make their next rocket even better. Want to do the same to yours? Of course you do. Turn the page and put your making-your-rocket-better skills to the test...

DID YOU KNOW?

THE SPACE CAPSULE SEPARATING FROM THE ROCKET BODY MID-FLIGHT IS EXACTLY WHAT HAPPENS WITH REAL SPACE ROCKETS. THE ROCKET-FUEL PARTS DETACH ONE BY ONE AS SOON AS THEY'VE BEEN USED UP.

CHAPTER FIVE
TESTING & TWEAKING

THIS IS WHERE THE REAL FUN BEGINS... Your rocket flew. Awesome. But did it fly exactly how you wanted it to? Are there things you would change? Of course there are! This is a perfectly normal part of engineering and it's when you get to really play with your rocket, test things out and make it the best it can possibly be. It's taken us about 800 years of "playing" with space rockets to get us to where we are today. Welcome to the engineering playground – trust me, it's a lot of fun.

NOT SURE HOW THIS WILL HELP...

YOU'LL SOON GET INTO THE SWING OF IT.

To start playing, firstly think about your rocket launch. You could get someone to help you record it (perhaps even in slow motion).

Did your rocket fly straight up?

Or did it fly off to one side or twist and flip in the air? Did your space capsule land with a thump?

However your rocket is flying, I have some tips to help you with testing and tweaking...

ASK AN ADULT TO HELP

TIP 1 ADD FINS

IF LAUNCHING YOUR ROCKET IS MORE "TUMBLE TIME" THAN "STRAIGHT LINE", ADDING FINS MAY BE THE ANSWER. FINS ARE STICKY-OUT BITS ON THE SIDES OF A ROCKET (A BIT LIKE THOSE ON A FISH – HENCE THE NAME) WHICH HELP TO KEEP IT FLYING STRAIGHT (THE ROCKET NOT THE FISH!).

PROBLEM

The way your rocket moves through the air is mostly down to its shape and weight. Your rocket is fairly large and light and so can be blown off track by the wind, or even just by the air as it flies through it.

SOLUTION

You need to give the air a larger area to push against at the bottom of the rocket than at the top. You can do this by adding fins. This means that when the top of the rocket starts to be blown off course, the air will push against the fins at the bottom of the rocket in the opposite direction, keeping the rocket straight.

WHAT YOU'LL NEED

- YOUR ROCKET BODY
- RULER
- TAPE MEASURE (A CLOTH ONE IS BEST)
- SCISSORS
- PEN
- ALL-PURPOSE GLUE

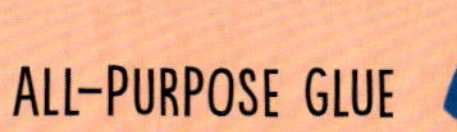

- STICKY TAPE

- 8 CM BY 12 CM SHEET (X2) OF THIN, STIFF PLASTIC OR WATERPROOF CARD (A CUT-UP MILK BOTTLE OR BUTTER TUB WORKS GREAT)

HERE'S HOW TO MAKE YOUR FINS:

1. Take one of the sheets of plastic and make a mark at 1 cm and 7 cm on both of the short edges.

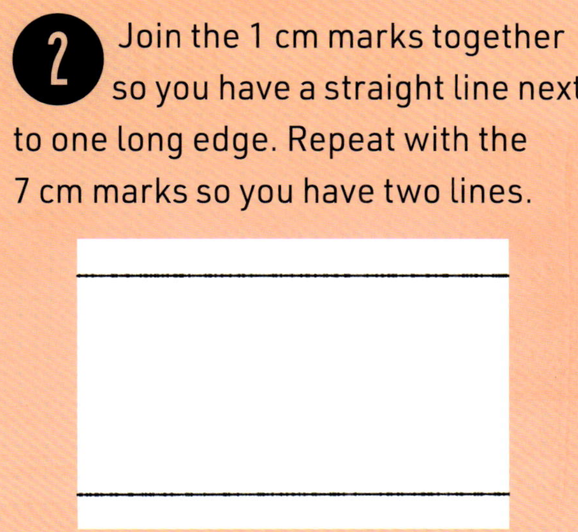

2 Join the 1 cm marks together so you have a straight line next to one long edge. Repeat with the 7 cm marks so you have two lines.

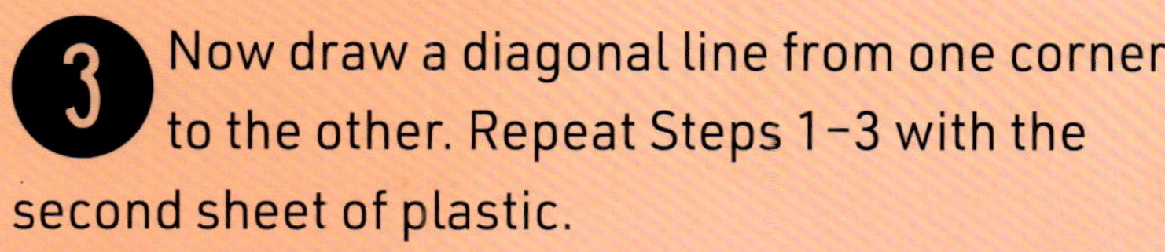

3 Now draw a diagonal line from one corner to the other. Repeat Steps 1–3 with the second sheet of plastic.

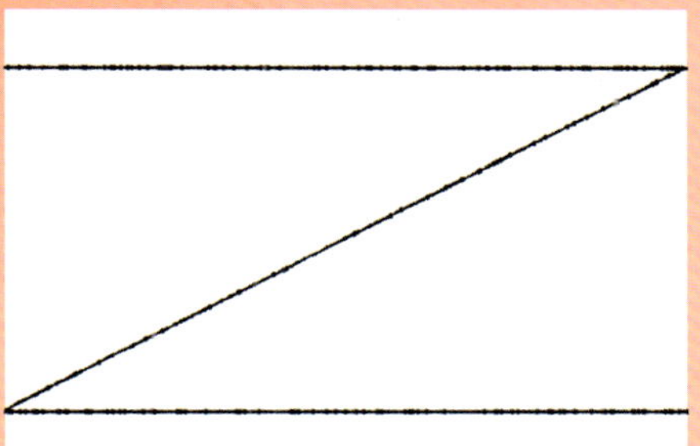

4 With an adult's help, cut along the diagonal lines on both sheets of plastic so you have four triangles with a flap. (You only need three, but keep one as a spare.)

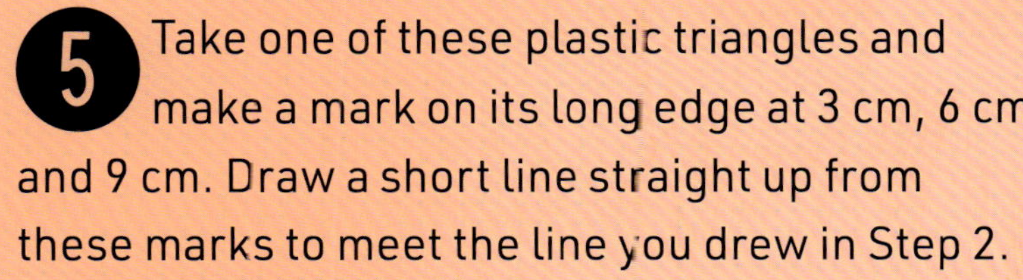

5 Take one of these plastic triangles and make a mark on its long edge at 3 cm, 6 cm and 9 cm. Draw a short line straight up from these marks to meet the line you drew in Step 2.

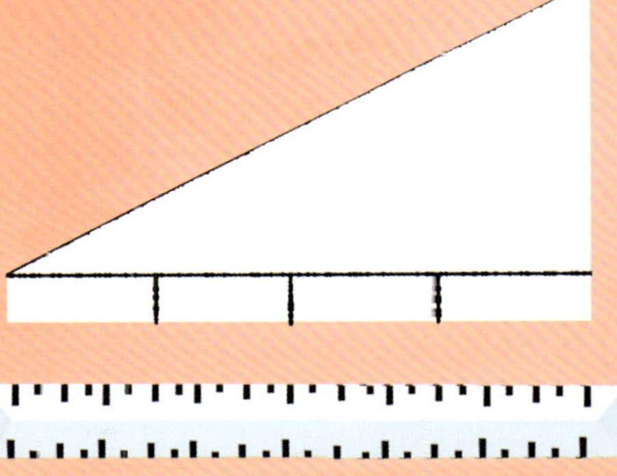

WHEN YOU'RE FIN-ISHED YOU'LL HAVE FINS LIKE MINE!

6. Cut along these three short lines so you now have four sections. Fold along the line you drew in Step 2, bending the first and third sections one way, and the other sections the other way, to make four flaps.

7. Repeat Steps 5–6 on the other triangles.

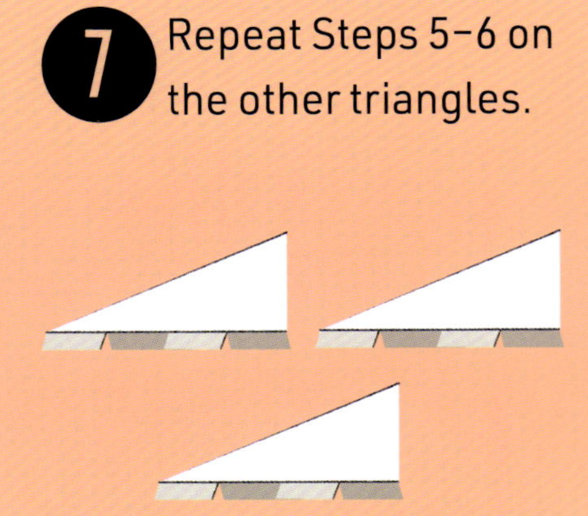

8. Now stand your rocket body on a table with the opening at the bottom, and hold your ruler straight up against the bottle. Make a mark on the bottle at 9 cm and 21 cm up from the table.

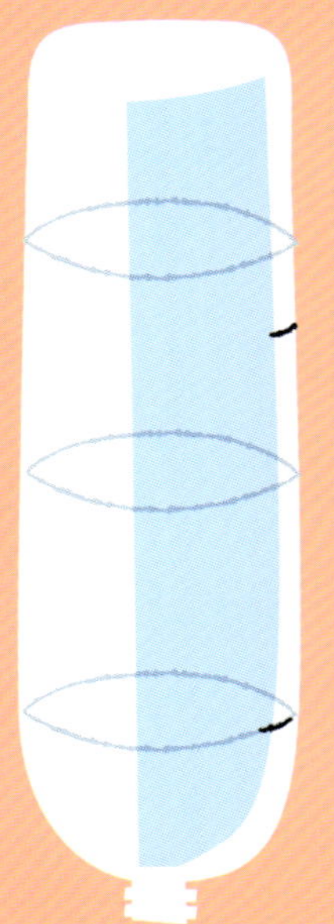

9. Wrap a tape measure around the bottle at both these points to draw two rings around the bottle.

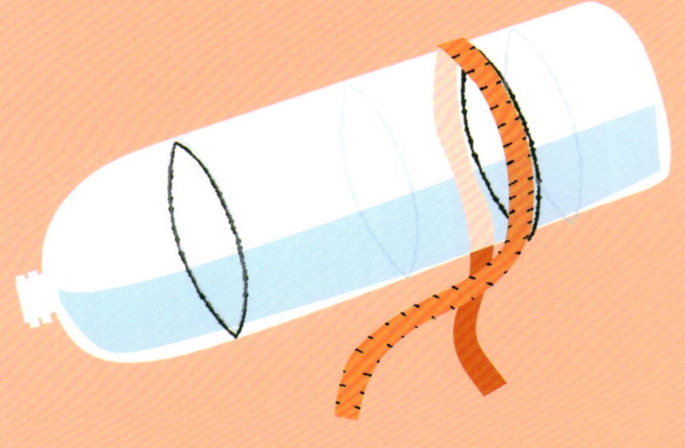

10. Turn the rocket body the other way up so its base is on the table. Hold the ruler against the bottle so it's straight. Using the ruler as a guide, draw a short line through each ring, making sure that the top mark is directly above the bottom mark.

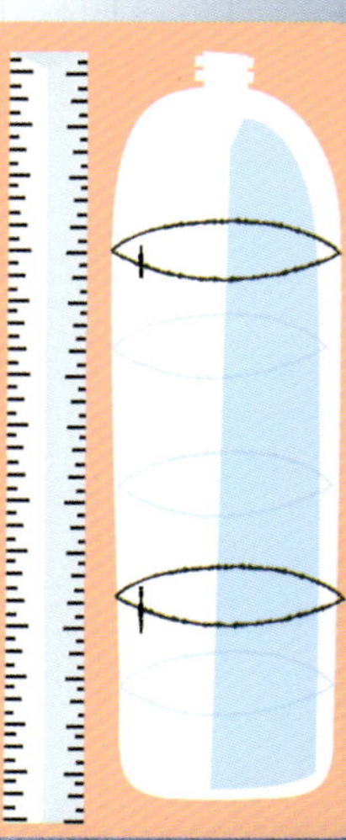

11 Place the tape measure around the bottom ring, then measure 10 cm from the mark and make another mark. Measure on a further 10 cm from this and make another mark. You should now have three marks on the bottom ring. Repeat for the top ring.

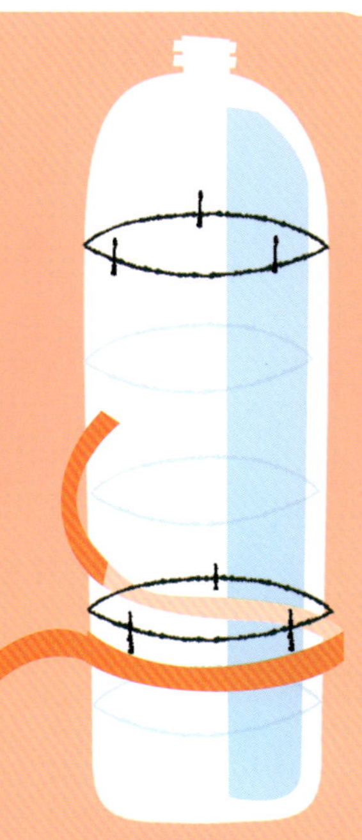

12 Turn the rocket so the opening is facing down. Line up one of your triangles with one pair of the marks you've just made, making sure the pointed bit is facing away from the bottle opening and the flaps are pressed against the bottle. Stick these flaps onto the bottle using glue, sticky tape or both.

13 Repeat Step 12 to stick two more triangles on the remaining marks on the bottle.

ASK AN ADULT TO HELP

TIP 2 CHANGE THE WEIGHT

ANOTHER WAY TO STOP YOUR ROCKET TUMBLING AND KEEP IT FLYING STRAIGHT UP (UNTIL IT COMES STRAIGHT BACK DOWN!) IS TO THINK ABOUT ITS WEIGHT. NOT JUST HOW HEAVY IT IS, BUT WHERE IT IS HEAVY.

WHAT YOU'LL NEED

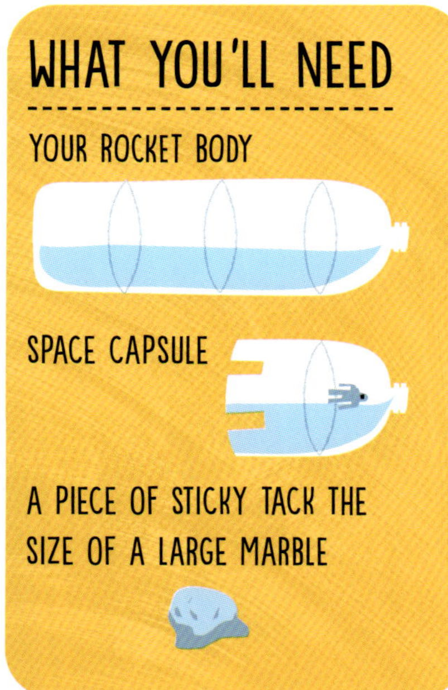

YOUR ROCKET BODY

SPACE CAPSULE

A PIECE OF STICKY TACK THE SIZE OF A LARGE MARBLE

PROBLEM

Our rocket is lovely and light so it can travel fast when it's launched. But once it's in the air, the rocket is so light that it can easily be blown off course. Adding fins does help to keep the rocket straight, but how do we stop the top of the rocket getting pushed around by the air so much?

SOLUTION

Weirdly, we need to add some weight, but not so much that it slows the rocket down. Making the top of the rocket heavier means it won't get blown around by the air so much. By using sticky tack, you can add the weight a bit at a time until you get the balance just right.

HERE'S HOW TO CHANGE THE WEIGHT:

1 Remove the space capsule from your rocket body.

2 Squash the sticky tack onto the top of the rocket body (which is the bottom of the bottle) so it's nice and flat.

3 Replace the capsule, ensuring that your mini toy person doesn't get stuck on the sticky tack. Launch your rocket again and see if it flies straighter. If not, add more sticky tack.

YOU CAN'T PUSH ME AROUND ANY MORE!

ASK AN ADULT TO HELP

TIP 3 ADD A PARACHUTE

WHAT GOES UP MUST COME DOWN, RIGHT? BUT IT DOESN'T HAVE TO COME DOWN WITH QUITE SUCH A THUMP, DOES IT?!

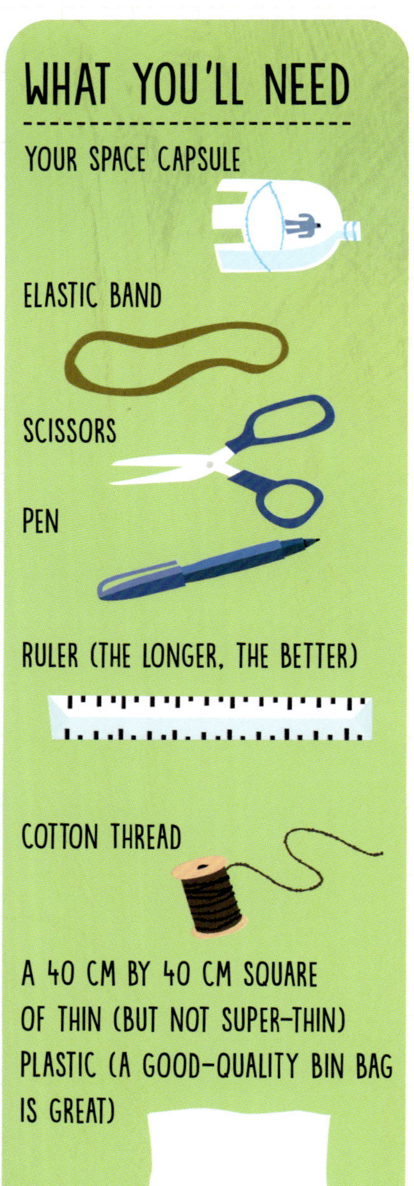

WHAT YOU'LL NEED

- YOUR SPACE CAPSULE
- ELASTIC BAND
- SCISSORS
- PEN
- RULER (THE LONGER, THE BETTER)
- COTTON THREAD
- A 40 CM BY 40 CM SQUARE OF THIN (BUT NOT SUPER-THIN) PLASTIC (A GOOD-QUALITY BIN BAG IS GREAT)

PROBLEM

Your mini toy person is having the adventure of their life. But when flying time is over they are hurtling back towards Earth and landing with such a bump it's enough to give even a toy person a headache!

SOLUTION

For your space capsule to gracefully glide back down to Earth, it needs something to catch the air as it falls. It needs a parachute. And yes, real space capsules also use parachutes when they are returning astronauts from their space adventures.

HERE'S HOW TO MAKE A PARACHUTE:

1 Take the sheet of thin plastic and fold it in half to make a rectangle. Then fold it in half again (but from the other side) to make a square.

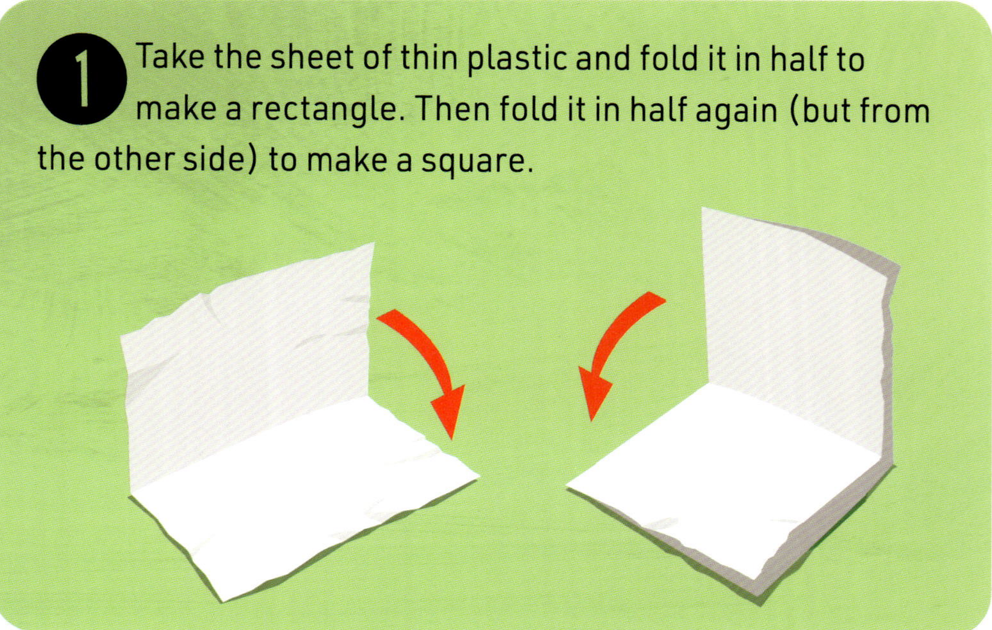

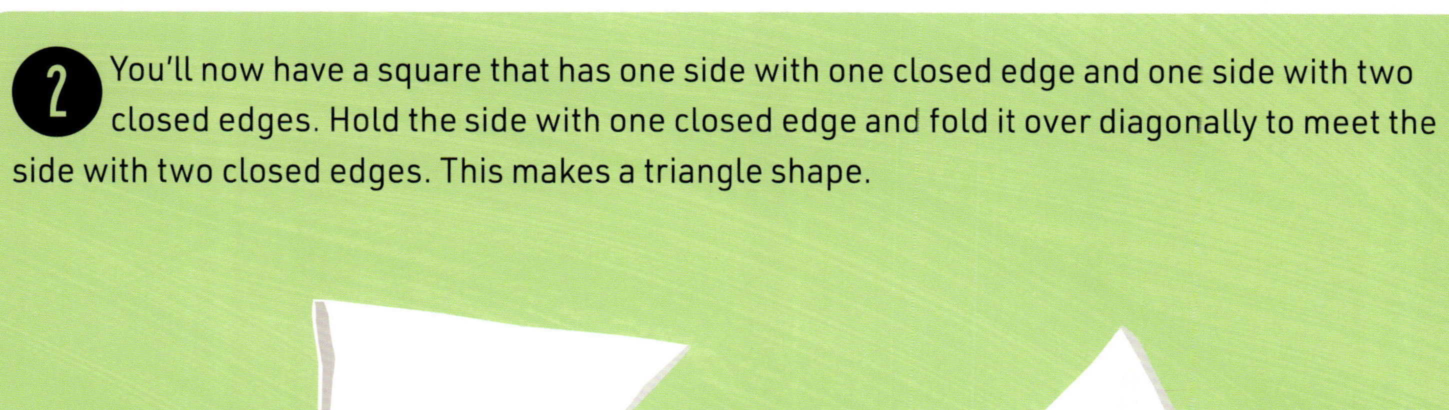

2 You'll now have a square that has one side with one closed edge and one side with two closed edges. Hold the side with one closed edge and fold it over diagonally to meet the side with two closed edges. This makes a triangle shape.

3 Make this triangle into an even slimmer triangle, by holding the side with one closed edge and folding it over to meet the side with three closed edges.

4 Flip this thin triangle over and, with an adult's help, cut off the extra bit of plastic as shown in the picture.

5 Now, on one of the long sides of the triangle, at the non-pointed end, measure 1 cm and 2 cm in from the short edge. Make a mark at each point. Repeat for the other long side of the triangle.

6 Draw a curved line between the 1 cm marks so that your triangle now looks like a slice of pizza.

7 With an adult's help, cut along the line you drew in Step 6.

8 On the side of the triangle with one closed edge, with an adult's help cut a small slit (about ½ cm long) at the 2 cm mark you made in Step 5. Only do this on the one side.

9 Now, at the pointy end of the triangle, cut off the very end of the point (only about ½ cm).

10 Open out your plastic sheet. You should now have a circle of plastic with eight small holes around its outside and one hole in its middle.

TOP TIP

THE HOLES MAY BE HARD TO SEE SO LOOK CAREFULLY!

11 Cut a piece of thread 40 cm long and thread one end of it through one of the holes around the outside of the circle. Tie securely using a triple knot, making sure you leave most of the thread loose. (It's fine to squash the small bit of plastic between the hole and the edge of the circle.)

12 Repeat Step 11 for the seven other holes around the edge of the circle.

13 Once all eight holes have thread attached, gather the loose ends together in one hand, and hold your plastic sheet in the other (grasping it around the middle hole). Making sure the threads aren't twisted, gently pull your hands apart so that all the threads are straight and tight.

14 Close to the end of the threads, tie them all together into one big knot.

15 Now tie the threads onto the elastic band, close to the knot you made in Step 14.

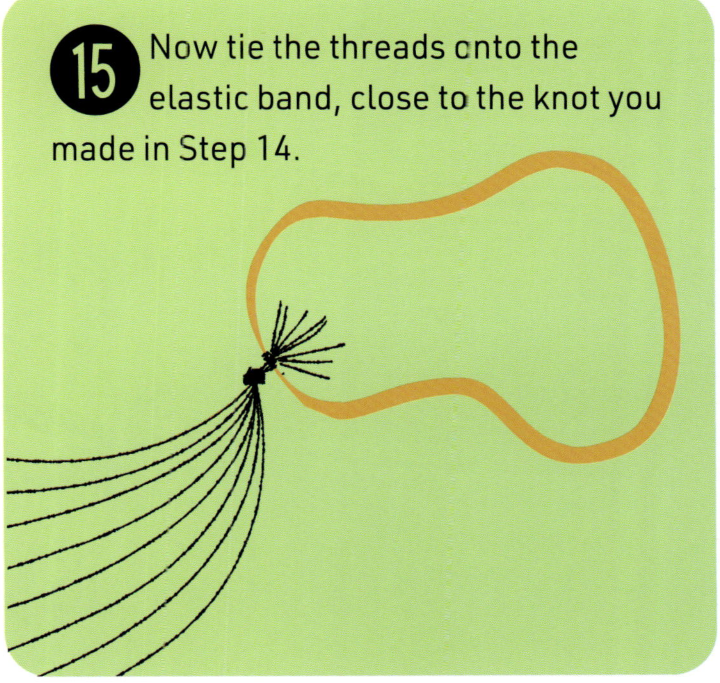

16 Wrap the elastic band around the bottle opening of the space capsule, making sure that it's tight enough to not slip off.

CHAPTER SIX

PERSONALIZATION

YOUR ROCKET IS BRILLIANT, SO LET EVERYONE KNOW IT'S YOURS BY PERSONALIZING IT. OF COURSE, IT'S TOTALLY UP TO YOU HOW YOU DO THIS, BUT I'VE INCLUDED SOME TEMPLATE IDEAS TO GET YOU STARTED. SO GET COLOURING, CUSTOMIZING AND CREATING!

MY NEW LOOK IS OUTTA THIS WORLD.

SOOO ROCKET 'N' ROLL!

TEMPLATES

TO USE THESE TEMPLATES, SIMPLY TRACE AROUND THEM ONTO PAPER, COLOUR THEM IN, CUT THEM OUT AND STICK THEM ONTO YOUR ROCKET OR LAUNCH PAD. TA-DA!

SPACE AGENCY LOGOS

ROCKET BODY PANELS

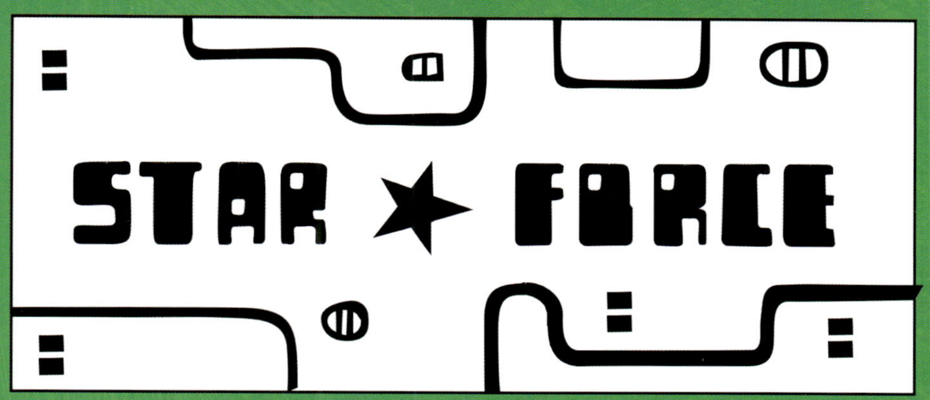

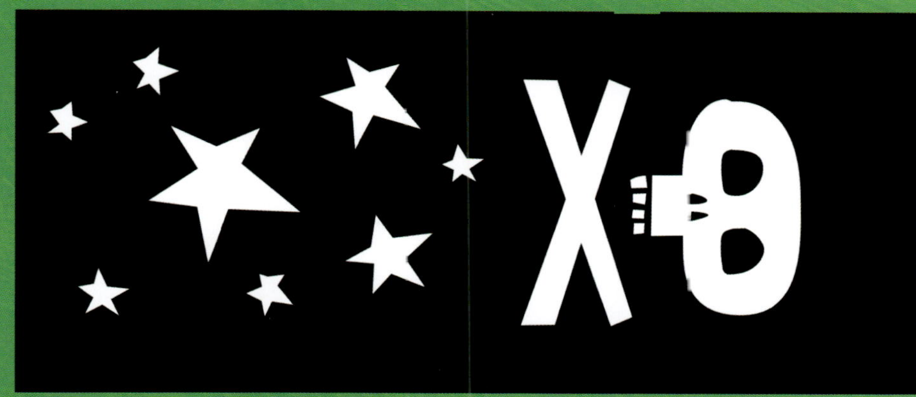

FIN TEMPLATES

PERFECT TO STICK ONTO YOUR FINS!

LAUNCH PAD TEMPLATE

GREAT FOR WRAPPING AROUND YOUR LAUNCH PAD.

BLAST OFF!

YOU NOW HAVE YOUR VERY OWN PERSONALIZED ROCKET WITH FINS AND A PARACHUTE. WELL, YOU DESERVE IT ALL, MY FRIEND!

But how do you launch your rocket with all these extra bits attached and make sure you fly into the sky, rather than tie yourself (and your rocket) in knots? Just follow these few extra steps...

1 Grasp your parachute by the middle hole. In your other hand, hold the capsule. If the threads are twisted, untwist them.

2 Gently squash the parachute into a thin sausage shape, by making your hand into a fist.

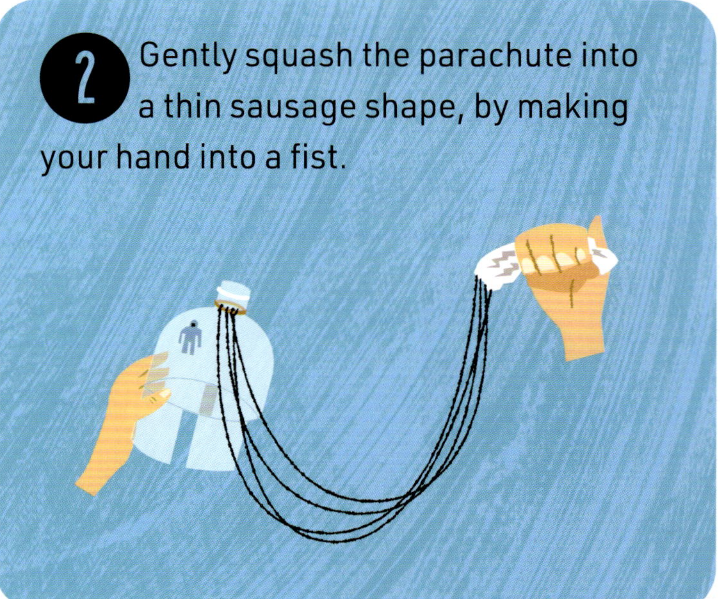

3 Post this squashed top bit of the parachute into the opening of the capsule, making sure it goes in no further than the elastic band. (Don't squash it all in – some should still be hanging out.) Now follow the launch steps as before (see pages 38–41).

As your rocket flies into the sky and your capsule gently falls back to the ground (and as you interview your tiny toy person about their time in space), you can smile to yourself – you just made an actual rocket! Make sure you save this book and your rocket in a special place, so when you next want to show off to someone, you know what to do.

It has been an absolute pleasure to be your guide on your first space mission. I know you're a kid right now, but even adults whose job it is to build huge space rockets were kids once. And I know for a fact that when they were kids, they would have built toy space rockets, just like you have done. So imagine, what could you be building in a few years' time?

I LOOK FORWARD TO LOOKING UP AND SEEING IT FLY BY.
BYE FOR NOW,

FRAN

TO MY AUNTIE GILL, AMY, CAITLIN AND OF COURSE GEOFF, WHOSE STAR STILL SHINES BRIGHTLY – F.S.

First published 2024 by Walker Books Ltd,
87 Vauxhall Walk, London SE11 5HJ

2 4 6 8 10 9 7 5 3 1

This book has been typeset in DIN

Printed in China

British Library Cataloguing in Publication Data: a catalogue record for this book is available from the British Library

ISBN 978-1-5295-0753-9

www.walker.co.uk

WALKER BOOKS
AND SUBSIDIARIES
LONDON • BOSTON • SYDNEY • AUCKLAND